GUNSMOKE MEMORIES

ALL RIGHTS RESERVED

ISBN: 9781098901110

For More Information, contact:

Jeff Hildebrandt

rangerhymer@hotmail.com

Gunsmoke Memories

Stories Behind the Story

Over the years, I've had the amazing good fortune to get to know some of my Gunsmoke heroes. Now, I'd like to share some of the inside stories they've told me about this ground breaking and history making series.

Special thanks to these who made Gunsmoke so entertaining:

James Arness	Dennis Weaver
Buck Taylor	Morgan Woodward
Martin Kove	Dean Smith
Ben Cooper	Don Collier
Mariette Hartley	Ed Asner
William Smith	Bruce Boxleitner

So, I hope you enjoy this. I really enjoyed talking with these folks and being able to share their memories.

A Gunsmoke Legacy

He's a Cowboy Legend from his hat to his boots.
He could ride like the wind.
He could rope and could shoot.
And, when we were young, on Saturday nights
we'd cheer as Matt Dillon would fight for the rights
of any lost soul who wandered his way.
And we swore that we'd all do
the same thing some day.
Matt Dillon, Chester,
Newly and Festus,
Doc and Miss Kitty;
you all really blessed us.

The good guys are gone and what's left us today
are heroes whose morals and feet are of clay.
So, I guess if young cowpokes are going to learn how
to respect one another, we have to start now
to teach them there's value in all that God's made,
to show love and compassion,
not anger and hate.
The young-ones need heroes to learn what to do
So, saddle up friend, 'cause that hero is you.

©Jeff Hildebrandt

Okay, let's begin. Dennis Weaver had been working on the movie, *Seven Angry Men,* when he got a call to audition for a new series at CBS.

"So, I went over and they gave me the sides for the character Chester and I read the sides outside in the hall, and to me the character was totally inane, absolutely stupid almost. And I thought to myself, well this isn't right, I'll try to straighten this character out. I'll use all my actor studio background, and I'll draw from myself and I'll use the method acting, so to speak, and I'll make this character straight and more reasonable and more understandable.
And when I read for it, you know, as an actor, after you finish reading, you always take a quick look at the director and producer to see how you've scored. When I looked at him, I knew I hadn't scored. Bill Warren said to me, 'Well Den I was hoping you would get a little more humor into the character.' And when he said that the light bulb went on and I remembered back at the University of Oklahoma when I was in the drama school. There was a kid that you could hardly understand when he spoke. I used to imitate him at parties and get a lot of laughs. I'd say things like "Eh let's get the dishrag and wipe under that baby's nose. If in there's nuthin' I can't stand, its nastiness.'
Or, 'Let's get the yungen in offen the street, she's out there nekkid as a jaybird, and that there, that Simpkin boy is taken it all in too.'
Well I thought about that and I said will you guys give me another chance? I think I have a key to the character. And so, I went out in the hall and I started reading the script with that accent.

Well it changed my whole psychology, my whole way of thinking. Actually, the script started making sense and it made me laugh actually. So, I went back in, and I read it with that accent and they just went right on the floor. And I could hardly get through the audition they were laughing so much."

Dennis didn't have to wait very long to find out the decision.

"The next day I was delivering flowers at George Barnes flower shop on Ventura Boulevard in the San Fernando Valley. The telephone rang, and the guy that owned it said 'Dennis, you're wanted on the phone. It's a guy named Charles Marcus Warren.
Well, it just scared me to death, you know,

I went to the phone trembling, not knowing what the situation was and picked up the phone and he said, 'Den, I just wanted to tell you, you got the part of Chester.' Oh man did I breathe a sigh of relief.

I tell you that was a moment. It was a turning point in my career, it really was, because that character, and believe me I thank God for Chester every day, it opened up my whole career and opened up doors for me. It really jump-started my career."

So, where did that stiff leg come from?

"When I first auditioned, I didn't use a limp. And one night after auditions for other actors, Bill Warren came up to me and said 'Den, can I talk to you after we finish here tonight?' And I said, 'What does he want, what have I done?' You know an actor is always scared that they're gonna lose the job for some reason.
So, he said, 'Would you mind acquiring some kind of a handicap with the character?'
And I said, 'Well, what do you want to do that for?'
He said 'Well ya see, historically and traditionally, a sidekick is always too old, or too young or too fat, or too something to get involved in all the physical stuff, you know, the fights and all that.
And we want you to be a nonviolent character. We don't want you to wear a gun. And because you are a leading man type physically, you just tried out for the 1948 Olympics in the decathlon, I don't want people writing in and saying 'Why doesn't Chester get involved more with the physical stuff?
So, if you would have some sort of a handicap, they wouldn't write in with those kinds of questions and I wouldn't have to answer them.'
I thought to myself, well that's a really kind of a strange reason for wanting an actor to develop a handicap. On the other hand, I was involved in different physical controls. That could be anything like a dialect or a headache or whatever it might be and it could be a handicap. I thought, well that's quite a challenge for an actor. And I love a challenge.

So, I went home and I decided that I had to have something that I could control easily, that I could make consistent so that people would actually believe that I really had the handicap. I thought to myself 'Well what if I just don't bend my knee? Maybe, if my knee is frozen.' And so, I hopped around the back yard for a couple a days over boxes and running and stooping and bending down and whatnot.

And it seemed to work. So, I went back to Bill the following day and I showed him the stiff leg and he said, 'Oh that's fine. That's fine. That's great! That'll do it. That'll do it.' He didn't care what kind of a handicap it was, just so he didn't have to write those letters.

But I tell you something, if I had known at the time that I was going to be walking stiff legged for nine years I might have had a different thought about it because, did you ever try and build a campfire stiff legged? Riding the horse wasn't too bad, but you ever try to put your boot on without bending your knee? I had to take yoga lessons to able to do some of this stuff. I had to be in really good shape to do that."

I'll get back to more stiff leg stories shortly. But, right now, let's go back to the beginning. Dennis was the first one cast and he helped audition the others, including those who wanted the part of Marshal Dillon. Ed Asner, who played in a couple of episodes, shared this story he heard about the auditions. I'm not saying it's true, but it's a cute story.

"I understood that they initially were going toward Denver Pyle but John Wayne called and said look at this guy who's worked for us, he's good. And Arness came in and they gave him the job. But prior to that they were having screen tests and they felt they were honor bound to do the same for William Conrad who played Dillon on radio. So, the test scene was that Dillon was sitting in his captain's chair behind the desk and this desperado comes through the door and says 'Dillon I'm gonna kill you.' And he reaches for his gun and Dillon bursts from the chair and shoots him dead. Well, when it came time for Conrad, the desperado comes through the door and says 'Dillon I'm gonna shoot you.'
Conrad rose to do his quick draw and the chair came up with him. I guess they decided to wait for Arness to come along."

Every Gunsmoke trivia fan knows that John Wayne declined the part, but I didn't know that James Arness had second thoughts until he told me this story:

"I actually had a pretty good part in a movie that I was doing and we were down in the Bahamas on location."

That movie, by the way was *Big Jim McLain*, with John Wayne. Sorry, I'll let Jim Arness tell the rest of his story now.

"They started calling asking when I was going to be back. It happened that the director of this movie, Eddie Ludwig was an old time pretty big movie director and I asked his opinion.

I said they want me for a Television series, you know a western series and he wasn't at all sure that this was something that I should do. He thought I should hang tough where I was. So, I was hesitant to take the show. Of course, I was under contract to John Wayne's company at this time and he heard I was having trouble deciding about it. So, he called me in and really gave me a feeling that I should do it. He said that it would be the best thing I could possibly do because I'd get to know how to handle myself in front of the camera and do all of the stuff that you have to learn. And, that all kinds of people would become familiar with me on screen and so forth. Well, I thought maybe I better take this guy's advice. Fortunately, I was at least smart enough to go ahead and take the part. So, that's actually how I wound up doing the thing. They called me in; we did a little test scene with Dennis and I and a heavy who comes into the scene.

And that was it; we started shooting the pilot a couple of weeks later I guess."

Arness gives credit to the writers for the success of the show.

"We had the great stories from the radio shows. And I'd say most of the shows that we did in the first few years were from the old radio scripts.

Later we started doing original stuff but to begin with we had all those great old stories which got us off to a fast start."

He adds that the Marshal Dillon character was clearly defined and he tried not to add too much of his own personality.

"Well, not consciously. I'm sure that had to be but I didn't consciously try, I was just playing the character the way it was written and I think probably when the camera stopped, I became somebody else. My real self you know. I couldn't have handled that job very long in real life you know. So, I think that's what it was."

Everyone agrees that the writing had a lot to do with the success. But Dennis Weaver says there was more to it than that.

"You know in a new pair of shoes; it gets easier as you break them in. They get more comfortable. And that's kinda the way it was with Chester and Doc and Matt. We began to work together so well, we began to ad lib, we began to improvise and we began to feel much looser.
The other thing was, when you're a number one show, for as long as we were. There was a period in time from our first show of the second season for four straight years we were number one, never off of that perch. It just builds your confidence; it just allows you to be looser and to grow and to experiment. The writers put Chester, in more interesting positions and situations. Brought in a girlfriend for him and just gave more interesting situations in which to display the depth and the breadth of that character."

Now, speaking of adlibs, Dennis looks back at the relationship between Chester and Doc.

"Well, Milburn and I just had a great working relationship. We ad-libbed a lot; we improvised a lot. And he was wonderful at it. Whatever I would feed him he would take and give it right back to me.

And of course, one of the running things on the show was I was always trying to get free medicine from him and always complaining too. I remember one time in a scene; I did a little line which I got from my mother. This is the actual truth.
She was from Arkansas down in the Ozarks and I got a lot of my character of Chester from her. And she would say things like, 'Oh, it's just really hurtin' today. It just feels like I got a butcher knife stuck in me and it's just a twistin' and a turnin.'
I remembered that line and one time I was walking down the streets in Dodge trying to get free medicine from him and I was 'Oh Doc I tell ya it's just like I got a butcher knife in me and it's just a twistin' and a turnin.'
Sometimes we'd break ourselves up and it was very difficult to get back into character and do the scene, because we just had such a good time laughing at each other. It was terrific."

Milburn Stone may be best remembered for the verbal ping-pong with Dennis Weaver and Ken Curtis, but Jim Arness says he meant much more to the show.

"He was a very special guy. He was born and raised back there in Kansas, not that far from Dodge City. And so, he had a real feeling for what it was like then.

In fact, when he was a young kid there were still some guys around, the old guys now that were sitting up on the boardwalk and whittling away and so on, and telling stories. They had actually been around during the days when some of this stuff was going on. So, he had a feeling for it, you know. And so, and he was very dedicated. He kind of took it on as his duty to make sure we didn't do anything that wasn't authentic. He really helped the show tremendously. I mean he was a guy who did have a lot of contribution to making it look just as real as possible. And he was also a great guy to work with. He kept you on the straight line. He didn't let you get off track at all."

One of Stone's biggest admirers was actor Ben Cooper, who said one particular episode stood out as one of the best working experiences of his career.

"It was called *Apprentice Doc* and I got to do 6 or 7 scenes, most of it was studying medicine with Milburn Stone.
And for an actor to work with Millie Stone was like somebody putting a million dollars in your pocket and saying I want you to feel secure. He was just fabulous. In it, talking about medicine, he was explaining how the civil war brought a lot of wonderful things to medicine. I said, 'The war?' He said, 'When there's death all around you, you learn how to try beyond yourself.'

And it's the first time, before or since, the only time I wrote a letter to an actor thanking him for the experience. And in it I said if I was at all good in our show, it's because you showed me so beautifully how to try beyond myself. I didn't tell the producers, but I would have paid them to let me do it."

I have to tell you here, that Ben Cooper was one of the nicest folks you'd ever want to meet. He was a favorite at Western film festivals around the country. I loved spending time with Ben and his wife, Pamela. They believed in encouraging everyone to be and to do their best.

There was another relationship that everyone seems to wonder about. You know the one I mean. What was up with Matt and Miss. Kitty? Dennis Weaver set the record straight.

"Well you know in the early days of television; we had some restrictions on what you could do. Censorship if you will. For instance, I remember that a man and wife that married could not sleep in the same bed. They always had twin beds. But Gunsmoke was the first adult western so we were supposed to have some leeway in terms of what we could do."

Dennis says a lot of viewers were curious about what sort of relationship those two had going on.

"We never really satisfied their curiosity because there was never any overt affection or lovemaking between the two.

And that was kind of interesting because I think it allowed people to use their imagination and to make the relationship whatever they wanted to make it. But you never in all the twenty years of that series, you never saw Matt Dillon kiss Miss Kitty. You saw 'em go upstairs but you never saw what happened when he went upstairs. So, you don't know. And that was part of the intrigue. That was part of what made it so interesting."

And he isn't a fan of today's style of movie making that doesn't leave anything to the imagination.

"They don't allow the audience to participate as the third party. And that, to me, is sad. One of the most effective movies that I ever made was a thing called *Duel*. And it was about the big semi chasing this guy in a little car, trying to kill him. There was no overt violence in that film, but yet people tell me it was one of the scariest movies that they ever saw. And it was all because they could use their imagination and what is going to happen was in their mind. They never saw it, it never happened. So, you know that's a long way of getting an explanation of that relationship between Miss Kitty and Matt Dillon, but that's what it was."

Did any of the cast lobby to consummate that relationship?

"No. You know, if it ain't broke don't fix it."

I guess while we're talking about Miss Kitty, I should let you know what Jim Arness said when I asked about Amanda Blake.

"Well, she was absolutely beautiful. But it's funny because I'm watching the old shows now and didn't realize how really great she comes across on the screen and what a fine actress she was.

She really did some acting on those parts and again she was exactly the right person for it, I can't imagine who else could have possibly played that, you know, she made the character totally her own.

Dennis Weaver says Amanda had a heart as big as a watermelon.

"She became Miss Kitty; she didn't want to do anything else after she got that part. She was a great lover of animals. She just cared so much about animals. One time I went down to where she lived in Scottsdale, Arizona. She had about a three acre back yard and every foot of that back yard was runs and cages and apiaries. She had about 25 jaguars back there because they were an endangered species.

She had bobcats up in her bedroom. She had birds, she had snakes. She just cared so much about animals. She was so sincere about it. A lot of people are not, you know, they put on a show. But not Amanda, her heart was like a big ole soft watermelon.

Olympic Gold Medalist, actor and stuntman, Dean Smith did a lot of work on Gunsmoke and told me how everyone felt about Amanda.

"Oh, what a great lady. She was always friendly to all of us. She was really nice to all the stunt people and all the horse people.

You could go up and talk to Amanda just very easily and she was very respectful to all of us guys. And she knew that if we were doing a stunt or something that we would look after her."

William Smith, who you'll remember from *Laredo* as well as that wonderful bare-knuckle fight with Clint Eastwood in *Any Which Way You Can*, got to see a slightly wilder side as they prepared for one episode.

"Well, the Gunsmoke I did, was a hell of a part. It was the first time on that show, Miss Kitty had never been raped and I raped her, tortured her and brought her back into town and James Arness beat me up."

Some folks think that episode called *Hostage* may be one of the best Gunsmoke's ever done. Smith says Amanda made sure he didn't pull any punches.

"The first thing I got to work, I walked on the set and I said, 'Where's Miss Kitty?'
They said she's right down there and I said 'Hi, I'm William Smith and I'm going to be playing Jude Bonner.'
She said I've been doing this show for 17 years and nobody's ever done me yet, now you do it right. And it embarrassed me so much I said what do you mean and she said you know what I mean."

Long after Gunsmoke ended, Buck Taylor and Dennis Weaver got back together at the Festival of the West. They hadn't seen each other in years.

As they renewed their friendship, there were some great Gunsmoke stories, like Buck talking about how he got the job as gunsmith, Newly O'Brian.

"It was a time in my early career. I'd been an actor 7 or 8 years before Gunsmoke, been under contract to Universal and so forth, but a lot of things happened to me all at once. I was about to be cast in a movie called *Hang 'Em High* with Clint Eastwood. Jack Lord requested me on *Hawaii 50* to play the part of Danno. I had done a Gunsmoke and they wanted to test me for a part of Newly. I tested with 5 different guys and I got the part and I had these 3 choices to make. Do you go with Hawaii 5-0, a brand-new show?

Do you go with Clint Eastwood or do you go with Gunsmoke? My gut feeling was Gunsmoke because I knew of the reputation that you all had as actors and as a family; an ensemble group of people that worked well together. I went with Gunsmoke and I don't regret it one bit."

And Buck shared how Gunsmoke keeps opening doors for other acting jobs.

"I did a movie a few years ago called *Tombstone.* I went in to read for a part and I noticed the director wasn't asking me to read.

He was telling me the story and at one point I thought I gotta stop this guy 'because I've been in there an hour and a half. I said, 'You want me to read for something' and he said 'No, I want you to play the part of Turkey Creek Johnson but I want you to read the script to see if you like it.' I got the part and then I asked him how he came to cast me in this movie? He said, 'I watched Gunsmoke every Saturday night in Wyoming, when I was a kid.' So, these are guys who are now running the movie business that are hiring us off Gunsmoke still."

Not only that, but Buck says playing Newly for 8 years provided a spring board for his other passion; art work.

"It was at this show that another artist came up to me and said, 'Do you want to do this and make a living?' I said 'Yes' and he said, 'When did you go on Gunsmoke?' I said 1967. He says, 'Since 1967, it's run once a week, twice a week, sometimes everyday somewhere in the United States. Find out where it's run the most and go there with your art work.' So, I did. I went to Fort Worth, to Kansas, to different places and the people showed up. I got press off it because I was kind of an interest, you know, a guy who paints from Gunsmoke. My work, I think, sold itself but I must say it's the Gunsmoke people that got me rolling."

Well, I promised I'd get back to Chester's stiff leg. Here's more from Dennis Weaver.

"I had a scene where I was in a buckboard with Miss Kitty and we were trying to get away from the bad guys. And we were hell bent for Dodge tryin' to get there. I told her I said, 'Miss Kitty, you go ahead I'm goin' to jump off here and hold off the bad guys.'

And I had a rifle in my hand and the buckboard was going as fast as the horses would go, probably eighteen, twenty miles an hour. And the producer said, 'We gotta get a double for you.' Well the first guy who ever doubled me in Hollywood was Richard Farnsworth, who later became a tremendous star in the movies. I said, 'Why don't we get Dick in here to do this doubling for me?' Richard, of course had never practiced stiff legged. He tried about four times coming down as fast as he could and jumping off the buckboard. He bent the leg every time because a stunt man is trained to cushion the blow and bend their knees. I finally said, 'Hey Dick, I'm sorry but this doesn't work. I guess I gotta do it. So, load up the buck board and let's roll.' I came down as fast as those horses would go. When I got to the right spot, I jumped off and my leg was out there sailing through the air. I got a lot of applause but I didn't bend the knee. A lot of people ask me, 'Did you have anything to keep from bending the knee?' And no, I didn't because I figured, if I was riding along and the horse went down, hit a gopher hole or whatever, I wanted the use of the leg in those situations.

And if I had some brace on there and the horse goes down, the stagecoach tips over or whatever I could have been in serious trouble. So, I didn't have anything, just muscle control."

Stuntman Dean Smith adds,

"I saw Dennis jump out of that wagon with one leg, and I've never seen a guy any more agile with one leg in my life.
But of course, a lot of people don't realize that Dennis was one of the great decathlon men in 1948. He missed making the `48 Olympic team by one spot. And I think the reason why, he was trying to audition in New York, for a part and maybe if he hadn't gone to that audition, he would have been on that `48 Olympic team. But then again he wouldn't have had the great career that he had."

Playing a character with a stiff leg on TV is one thing. But taking it to the streets is another. Dennis says to promote the show, he, Milburn Stone and Amanda Blake went to fairs and rodeos where they entertained as the "Gunsmoke Trio."

"Milburn Stone was brought up in tent shows and Vaudeville and he just loved to sing and to perform, and he also loved money.
He thought why don't we start a thing called the Gunsmoke Trio. I'll never forget in a rodeo arena, with the lights down low and the first one out was Milburn Stone. He walked out to the stage, stood there, sucked his teeth, tipped his hat, and said, 'Folks, I wanna sing one for all us old folks.'
And he sang, 'When You and I Were Young Maggie,' and I tell ya there wasn't a dry eye in the house.

Then he brought out Amanda Blake, and they did a little routine together and then finally he said; 'Now folks, I know who you're all waiting for, and here he is out of shoot number one, Our Chester!'
Well it was the greatest introduction I ever had. The spotlights go over to shoot number one. Now, what does the audience expect? They expect Chester to come barrelin' outta there on a horse, you know and doing his thing. The gate opens up, and I come running outta there, no horse. I had some things set up so that I had to jump over. They were actually low hurdles that we ran in track. And I would jump over those low hurdles, stiff legged, and land on the stage and I'm tellin' you the applause was absolutely thunderous. It was probably one of the most exciting intros that any actor ever had."

But Dennis says he couldn't do the soft shoe routine with Milburn and Amanda, so he came up with a way to get rid of the stiff leg on stage. While sitting on a short stool he'd pick up a guitar and try to play it. Well, the guitar kept sliding down his stiff leg. He'd do that several times and then tell the arena crowd,

"Well folks, I think its time that I was just real honest with ya."

Then he'd bend his knee and kick his leg straight out.

"And it just went bananas. So, from then on, I didn't have the stiff leg in the show and we'd do a soft shoe routine and a lot of jokes and small patter. It was great.

We were the most sought-after act on that circuit. And the number one act was none other than Roy Rogers.

Now, let's get some insight into Jim Arness. He left a lasting impression on the actors who shared the screen with him.
While we were at one of the Tombstone Film Festivals, Don Collier shared this memory of working with Arness in the episode "The Promoter."

"He hated dialog. He'd take his script and he'd rip off his dialog and he'd have 2 or 3 little pieces in his hand, do about 3 lines in one take. They'd say cut and he'd rip out 3 more, you know. He hated dialog; he didn't like it at all."

William Smith had a similar experience with Arness in an episode called "Hard Labor"

"James Arness and I did one show where we were in a cave together. It was the last Gunsmoke ever done, and he didn't like to do a lot of lines and I was playing a crazy guy."

He did a little imitation that, frankly, would not be considered politically correct by today's standards. Then went on,

"and he gave me all his lines, and we sat down there for 3 days in this cave and shot that show and that was the last one done."

And just so you don't think their experience was a fluke, Sherree North had this to say about her appearance in an episode titled "Lover Boy."

"So, he'd rip out the pages of that scene. He'd get on that horse. The pages were just out of camera. You'd finish speaking and he was looking at the lines down here. Then he'd look back up and just shoot 'em to you. That's sort of how we'd do the scene with James. Then he'd get off the horse and the first thing, all that heavy belts and guns and all that stuff would drop to the ground and he'd walk to his chair in the shade."

Then there is Bruce Boxleitner who showed up in the last season. He really got to know and appreciate Jim Arness later as they worked together in the TV series, *How The West Was Won*.

"Jim was always kind of like my mentor, and just by example, I watched how the lead in a television series behaves and how you handle the day in and day out. Some people don't do it at all very well, they're terrors in fact and we hear about them. But there are people like he was who welcomed guest stars personally, sat and talked with you, enjoyed doin' the material and no temper tantrums."
Bruce says that if there ever was something wrong, Arness would always deal with it away from the cast and crew. "Because the morale of the day's work starts from the top and works its way down.
If Jim was having' a bad day then everybody would be havin' a bad day, you know what I'm sayin', work-wise."

This is how Arness reacted to Boxleitner's impression:

"I didn't consciously try to assert any control. That's not really my nature, I guess. And things were going so well that there wasn't ever any reason to start inserting my opinions. Again, that's one of the reasons it lasted so long because you can have the best stories and the best actors and all, but if there's conflict between the people you can't go on year after year doing that."

Let me get back to Don Collier for a minute. He told me another story that happened while he was on a series called *The Outlaws*.

"The second year, a guy named Bruce Yarnell came in and played the deputy. Bruce was 6 foot 7, big guy. The first week he was there, they were shooting Gunsmoke in the stage next to us and I know he thought maybe he was bigger than Jim Arness. He says, 'Listen Don, you know Jim. How about taking me over to the stage and introducing me to him.'
I knew what he wanted to do, so I was more than happy to accommodate him. We walked in and they're shooting the scene. Jim was standing there and man he was big. Bruce stopped and he kinda eye-balled old Jim and he says, 'Well he's busy, maybe we better not bother him.'"

Collier says they both just went back to their own stage.

Dennis Weaver actually got a little choked up thinking back about Arness.

"Jim Arness, man he's one of the great, great guys I've ever had the pleasure and the privilege of working with. He's the salt of the earth. What you see is what you get.

There's no phoniness about Jim whatsoever and I'll tell ya something, he could spot a phony that came on the set quicker than anybody, I don't know, he had an innate sense of character and he wouldn't have anything to do with 'em. But the guys who were honest with him he was wonderful, he was such a loyal person, and such a caring and compassionate person.

As a matter of fact, we had a hairdresser on the set that developed cancer and he made sure that all of her hospital bills were taken care of. He was a very giving person."

"I always thought of him as an onion. You see something on the outside, but it's not nearly what he is on the inside. You peel off one layer of the onion and you get something else. And if you go deep enough with Jim and you peel off enough layers, you get down to the core of what Jim is. And his center is love really. He is very understanding, very compassionate, very concerned about you. He's a guy that just wears well. I can't say enough about him. I have such great respect for him and what he's done.

Speaking of being at the core of something, Dennis was at the core of one of the first big hurdles the show had to face. Jim Arness remembered what it was like when Dennis left the show.

"He said he was going to leave ahead of time so we knew he was leaving, but I don't think anybody felt comfortable about it. We were on such a roll that why fool with something that's successful, you know. And we all were wondering what would happen at this point. You just take him out of the show and what happens?"

But Arness says director Andy McLaglen had worked with a young guy named Ken Curtis.

"He decided to bring this character in for one show to try it out and he just seemed to feel right. So, when Dennis left, they had him ready to step in and man it worked out great. He was able to add pretty much all the comedic stuff that Dennis had but in addition to that they had him doing, many more serious character things. We lucked out."

One of the things I enjoy about watching Gunsmoke is the endless parade of guest stars. I mentioned that to Jim Arness who told me,

"Many actors who later became highly successful actors were on the show through the years. In later years, they decided to bring in people who had been big names, like Bette Davis and they seemed to be willing to come on. It's a part of what kept it going, I think."

Dennis Weaver says they had actors lining up around the block to be on the show.

"I think everybody in Hollywood passed through Gunsmoke at one time or another."

Dennis adds that one reason the show was so popular with actors was they way they were treated by the rest of the cast.

"When a guest actor came on the Gunsmoke set they were treated as part of the family. We respected the talent of all those actors simply because we knew that the show depended upon their performance and what they could give."

One of those guests was Ed Asner.

"I was close to being an unknown when I came in as a guest performer and they couldn't have been nicer. One of the shows I did I was a drunken, treacherous cavalry sergeant who pulled a knife in a bar fight. Dillon threw me in the jug to sober up over the weekend. So then, it's time to let me out of the jail and I come out and try to blind side him with a haymaker. He blocks it and punches me out. I just felt so ridiculous. I mean there he was up there. And here I am. No man in his right mind would have ever taken a swing at Jim Arness.

I felt ridiculous doing it but went through the motions and nobody laughed. That's how dignified they were, that's how easy they were."

While I'm on the subject of guest stars, I asked Dennis if he had any favorites.

"My favorite guest star of course was Struther Martin, who played in a show called *Cooter.* That was the first episode that got number one ranking nationally. So Struther Martin was obviously great.
I'll tell you another person that was interesting. It was a guy named Aaron Spelling. Aaron Spelling had an acting part on Gunsmoke, and he came into town riding a donkey and playing a guitar. And the first person that befriended him was Chester.

Another star who shines brightly in Dennis' memory is Jack Elam who played in one of the episodes Dennis directed.

"I had the good sense to know that half of the director's job was casting the right actors. But I'll tell you the thing about Jack; don't ever play liar's poker with him. You know what that is? You pull out a dollar bill, and you bet on the hand.
Every dollar bill's got numbers on it. And if you've got three of a kind, that's good. You've got full house, that's good. You've got four of a kind, of course that's the best. But Jack Elam always kept a secret dollar bill in his wallet someplace that only he knew where it was and it was a real powerhouse hand. And when the money got high and the stakes were big, he'd just pull out that dollar bill. So, you had to be careful with Jack, he was a wily person."

Gunsmoke may have been considered a "drama" but the cast sure seemed to have a lot of fun. Buck Taylor says it got to the point where he couldn't work with Jim Arness.

"He's a funny guy. I couldn't look him in the eye. I'd be serious and he'd make me laugh, so that was a big problem with me on Gunsmoke. I was always running into the Marshal's office and saying, 'There's a fight in the Long Branch!' and he'd go, 'So what?'"

Dennis says some of the funny incidents that happened with Jim Arness were totally unplanned.

"We were shooting Gunsmoke at Melody Ranch. You know you do the master scene and you get to the close up. When we would shoot his close up, he would have his hand behind him and as soon as he got through talking, he would come around with an ice cream cone and start licking it. So, you never could cut to him except when he was talking.

They finally brought him in to the projection room one day and said, Jim we want you to look at what you're doing. Well he was so embarrassed, he never did it any more."

Morgan Woodward has the distinction of being a Gunsmoke guest star more than any other actor.

"In one segment, Arness was waiting at my ranch house for me and the ranch house was up on a hill. If you remember Jim was 6' 6" and a half.

Well, in those days I was 6' 3" so I was no runt. I saw Arness up on the hill at my house waiting for me and that kind of upset me because I didn't have a lot of love for Marshal Dillon. The director staged it so that I rode up the hill got off my horse and walked up to Arness and started giving him what for. Well he said okay let's shoot it. So, I rode up the hill got off my horse and walked up to Arness and all of a sudden, I realized that I was talking into his fly.

I started laughing and said are you sure you want to continue this shot; you know I'm talking into his fly. That broke up the cast so we restaged it. I rode a little further up the hill got off and walked down the hill so I could at least look him in the eye."

Now, Mariette Hartley is no stranger to acting. She came from what they call legitimate theater. As a matter of fact, she started performing Shakespeare when she was 10 years old.

"And I suddenly ended up in Hollywood and thought I had died and gone to hell."

Her first experience in a Western was *Ride the High Country*.

"But Gunsmoke was my very first television show and it was a gorgeous piece of writing. Kathleen Hite had written it called *Cotter's Girl*. It was the story of a young girl who was raised by an alcoholic father and it was so interesting because it was kind of parallel to my life."

But that episode sticks with her because of fun they had on the set.

"These guys are legendary; these guys cannot look at one another without laughing. I don't know if you know that. All Dennis would have to do is walk and Jim would be gone.
Once Jim went, Millburn Stone went and Amanda Blake went. Once those four people went, there was no way you could walk through their laughter. You couldn't even move through their laughter. So, we had a scene where I had to be taught how to eat. And they served me a steak and I had no idea how to cut the steak so I shoved the full steak in my mouth. Now Jim never read the entire script; he read one page at a time. Read it, memorize it, rip it up and throw it away. He had no idea what I was gonna do. The minute I picked up the steak and shoved it in my mouth and couldn't get it down they were gone. By the time we finished, when they were frying that steak in the kitchen they started to laugh. And it just went from bad to worse to worse to worse. We started that scene at four O'clock in the afternoon. We got that scene the next day at 11:30 in the morning. I have never laughed so hard in my life.

They would finally have to separate them. They'd put Dennis in his trailer. Then Jim would do his lines to the script person, who didn't make him laugh and vice, versa. It's the only way they could get the whole series done. It was great."

**Here's another Don Collier story from his days on
The Outlaws. You remember his set was next to the
Gunsmoke set and he would sneak over there for
lunch. Well, not really lunch. Lunch was just an
excuse to play cards.**

"We'd play either hearts or pinochle. But Jim and
Dennis were vegetarians. That was the only thing I had
against them. They'd eat this alfalfa sprouts and all that
crap and we went right along with them because they
were a lot bigger stars than we were and we'd say sure
we love that stuff and we'd eat that garbage and play
cards. It was a lot of fun."

**Of course, Dennis remembers those card games and
how they even included Jim's stand in, Tiny Nichols.**

"Well Jim's not a great card player, but he was
determined. And so, we'd play in between scenes while
they were lighting the set.
Well, first of all, the actors would block it. We would
determine where the moves were and etcetera."
And then they would say 'Ok, we're ready for the second
team,' which means the stand-ins were supposed to go
in and mimic what we had done as actors. Well, of
course, we would get in a card game, the three of us,
very quickly after the principles were finished with
blocking the scene. Well, Tiny would be in a game with
us and if Jim had a good hand he'd say 'Sit down Tiny, sit
down. Don't pay any attention. Let the second assistant
stand in, let him do it. I want to play this hand.' Time
and time again they'd call for Tiny and he'd be in a card
game with us.

And finally, they hired a stand in for the stand in. And Tiny Nichols, as a stand in for Jim Arness had his own stand in so we could play cards."

Dennis says they played just about every lunch break.

"We'd go up to Jim's room because he'd send Tiny up ahead to fix his lunch and get ready so we could get right into the card game. And we'd walk into the room and Jim would go to the cupboard where he kept his little marble bag. It was always full of quarters. He'd replenish it every day.

He'd get this bag of quarters out of the cabinet and he'd throw it on the table and he'd say 'OK you S. O. B.'s, get that!' And by the time lunch was over, we'd have it. One time he said to somebody, 'You know, I paid for Dennis' pool.' He did pay for part of it, at least the diving board."

Morgan Woodward has another story about Jim Arness from the first show of the last season, called *Matt Dillon Must Die*.

"Marshall Dillon had shot one of my sons and my sons and I were after him. We were gonna give him 30 minutes and we were gonna take after him with our dogs."

Well, they caught him. And what happened next is the sort of story that bounces from one cocktail party to the next.

"Victor French directed this and thought it'd be great for me to be sitting in a rocking chair watching Matt Dillon dig his own grave. Now where he came up with that rocking chair up in the mountains I don't know.

Anyway, I was sitting there in that rocking chair watching Matt Dillon dig his own grave. And the dialogue was that I said 'Alright Dillon that's deep enough. You got any last words?' And Matt was supposed to say, 'You'll never get away with this. The law will track you down. You'll live to regret it.' So, I watch Dillon dig for awhile and I say, 'Alright Dillon that's deep enough. You got any last words to say?' And Jim takes off his hat and looks skyward, and he says, 'The lord giveth and the lord taketh away. And if that ain't a square deal I'll kiss your ass.'
We didn't get back to filming for a half hour."

Ed Asner feels that along with the laughter, Gunsmoke left a serious legacy of dealing with important social issues.

"Let's say civil rights or racial or religious discrimination. There were two ways to introduce it into TV in those days, either through science fiction or through Westerns. I think Gunsmoke was brilliant in that it dealt with discrimination, it dealt with morals that people in those days didn't have the guts to do.

So, they dealt with humanity, which you don't find too much of on TV these days. Because humanity takes more than a thirty second sound bite."

A lot has changed since September, 1955. Our world is racked with violence and blind hatred. What we need is a refresher course in tolerance, love and respect. We need to stand against injustice to ensure the survival of the rights and values this country was founded on.

We need a lot less bloodshed and a lot more Gunsmoke.

Well, there you have it. I know there are a lot of Gunsmoke books out there. Ben Costello wrote a great one called "Gunsmoke: An American Institution." And if you want to know about Miss Kitty, I'd suggest, Becky Burgoyne's, "Perfectly Amanda, Gunsmoke's Miss Kitty, To Dodge and Beyond." They are certainly more in-depth. But I just wanted to share these memories from the actors who kept us coming back to Dodge City every week. Thanks for taking this ride with me. I hope you enjoyed it.

Jeff Hildebrandt

Made in the USA
Las Vegas, NV
16 April 2024

88773264R00023